How to Draw the Life and Times of
Lyndon B. Johnson

Melody S. Mis

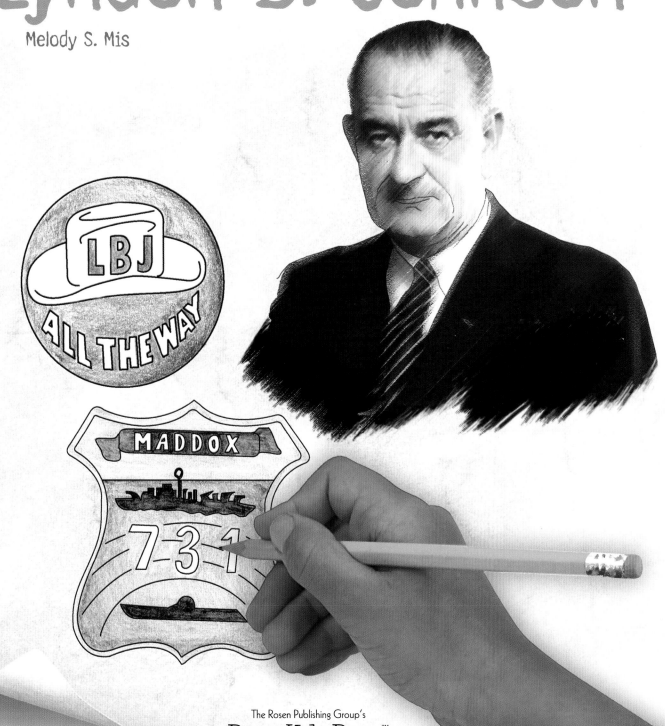

The Rosen Publishing Group's
PowerKids Press™
New York

To Roberta and Otis Parkman for being part of our family

Published in 2006 by The Rosen Publishing Group, Inc.
29 East 21st Street, New York, NY 10010

First Edition

Editor: Jennifer Way
Layout Design: Ginny Chu
Photo Researcher: Jeffrey Wendt

Illustrations: All illustrations by Albert Hanner.
Photo Credits: pp. 4, 16 LBJ Library photo; p. 7 LBJ Library photo by Cecil Stoughton; p. 8 LBJ Library photo by Charles Bogel; pp. 9, 10 Garren Zuck/presidentialavenue.com; pp. 12, 22 © Bettmann/Corbis; p. 14 Library of Congress Prints and Photographs Division; p. 18 U.S. Senate Collection; p. 20 Lyndon B. Johnson National Historical Park; p. 24 Naval Historical Center; p. 26 NASA Marshall Space Flight Center; p. 28 LBJ Library photo by Arnold Newman.

Library of Congress Cataloging-in-Publication Data

Mis, Melody S.
How to draw the life and times of Lyndon B. Johnson / Melody S. Mis.— 1st ed.
p. cm. — (A kid's guide to drawing the presidents of the United States of America) Includes index.
ISBN 1-4042-3012-2 (library binding)
1. Johnson, Lyndon B. (Lyndon Baines), 1908–1973—Juvenile literature. 2. Presidents—United States—Biography—Juvenile literature. 3. Drawing—Technique—Juvenile literature. I. Title: Life and times of Lyndon B. Johnson. II. Title. III. Series.
E847.M56 2006
973.923'092—dc22
2005014681

Printed in China

Contents

Lyndon Baines Johnson

Lyndon Baines Johnson was a teacher, a congressman, a senator, and a U.S. president. He is known as one of the smartest politicians of his time. Johnson was born on August 27, 1908, on a ranch near Stonewall, Texas. He was the first of five children born to Sam Ealy Johnson Jr. and Rebekah Baines Johnson.

Johnson graduated from high school in 1924, and he went to California to work. Johnson returned to Texas in 1926, and a year later he entered Southwest Texas State Teachers College in San Marcos. He graduated from college in 1930, and he got a teaching job in Houston, Texas.

In 1931, Johnson moved to Washington, D.C., after Democratic congressman Richard Kleberg asked him to become his secretary. On a visit to Austin, Texas, in September 1934, Johnson met Claudia Alta Taylor, whom he married fewer than two months later. The Johnsons had two daughters, Lynda and Luci.

In 1937, Johnson won a special election to take the place of a Texas congressman who had died in office. He served in the House of Representatives for five terms, from 1937 to 1949. He then left Congress to serve in World War II from December 1941 to July 1942.

In 1948, Johnson was elected to the U.S. Senate, where, in 1955, he became the Senate majority leader. Johnson was known in Congress as a man who could get people to compromise. When John F. Kennedy ran for president in 1960, he chose Johnson as his vice president. Kennedy and Johnson won the election.

You will need the following supplies to draw the life and times of Lyndon B. Johnson:

✓ A sketch pad   ✓ An eraser   ✓ A pencil   ✓ A ruler

These are some of the shapes and drawing terms you need to know:

Horizontal Line	—	Squiggly Line	
Oval		Trapezoid	
Rectangle		Triangle	
Shading		Vertical Line	
Slanted Line		Wavy Line	

The Thirty-sixth President

When President John F. Kennedy was assassinated on November 22, 1963, Vice President Lyndon Johnson became the nation's thirty-sixth president. Johnson continued the projects that Kennedy had started and also started some of his own programs.

During the 1964 presidential race, Johnson talked about his vision for the government to help the poor. He called his vision the Great Society. As part of his Great Society, Johnson declared a "war on poverty."

Johnson won the 1964 presidential election. By 1967, Johnson had passed about 200 major new laws. One of the most important of these laws was the Voting Rights Act of 1965, which ensured the voting rights of African Americans.

Johnson's popularity did not last. America's part in the unpopular Vietnam War had increased under his leadership. Many American soldiers had been killed, which angered people in the United States. His falling popularity led Johnson to decide not to run for reelection in 1968.

Lyndon Johnson was sworn into office aboard *Air Force One* on November 22, 1963. *Air Force One* is the airplane the president uses. Kennedy's wife, Jacqueline, stands to Johnson's left.

Johnson's Texas

The Lyndon Baines Johnson Library and Museum is at the University of Texas at Austin. The library opened in 1971.

Texas

Map of the United States of America

Lyndon Johnson loved his home state of Texas. Even when he was president and living in Washington, D.C., Johnson returned to his Texas ranch as often as he could. This earned the ranch the nickname the "Texas White House." Because of his ties to the state, the Lyndon Baines Johnson Library and Museum was built at the University of Texas at Austin. The library's displays tell about Johnson's life and his presidency. There are gifts that were given to Johnson when he was president, his car, which was a 1968 Lincoln limousine, and a small model of his office in the White House. The library is open to the public.

Lyndon Johnson is buried in his family's cemetery. It is part of the Lyndon B. Johnson National Historical Park.

Near Austin, in the town of Stonewall, is the Lyndon B. Johnson National Historical Park. The park includes Johnson's reconstructed birthplace, the first school he attended, the ranch where he and Mrs. Johnson lived, and the family cemetery. After Johnson died in 1973, he was buried in the family cemetery. His gravestone is easy to find, because it is the tallest one in the main section of the cemetery.

After the Johnsons donated part of their ranch to the U.S. government in 1972, it became part of the Lyndon B. Johnson National Historical Park. People can visit the park today to learn more about the thirty-sixth president.

Johnson's Birthplace

Lyndon Johnson was born in a small house on his grandfather's farm near Stonewall, Texas, on August 27, 1908. His grandfather Sam  Ealy Johnson Sr. had built the home in 1889. The Johnsons lived in the house from 1907 until 1913, when they moved to Johnson City. It was at Johnson's birthplace that he learned to read at age four.

Since the Johnsons could not make a living from the farm, they sold it in 1922. The home was torn down in the 1940s. Johnson had such wonderful memories of his childhood home that he purchased the property in 1951. He had his birthplace rebuilt in 1964. The builders were able to use some of the lumber and fireplace stones from the original house.

The rebuilt birthplace home is located on the grounds of Johnson's ranch. When he was president, Johnson used the home as a guest cottage for visitors. Today the birthplace is part of the Lyndon B. Johnson National Historical Park and is open to the public.

1

Begin the drawing of the house with a rectangle.

2

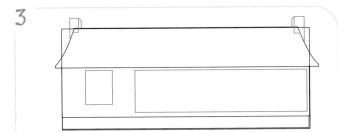

Next draw the base of the house by making a long rectangle at the bottom. Add a bigger rectangle on top of that. Then draw the shape of the roof of the house.

3

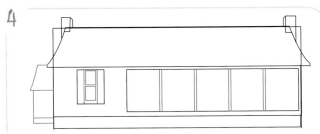

In the middle of the house draw the rectangle for the window on the left. On the right draw the large rectangle where the front porch will be. Then draw chimneys on both the far left and the far right sides of the roof.

4

Draw the addition off to the left side of the house as shown. Add the panes to the window using vertical and horizontal lines. Then draw the four posts in the large rectangle for the front porch.

5

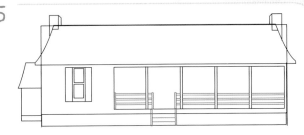

Now draw the railing on the front porch. Start with the vertical posts and then draw the horizontal ones. Add lines for the steps.

6

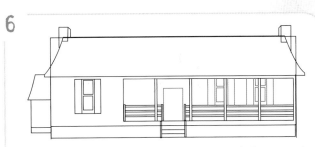

Draw the windows that are behind the porch. Then draw the front door.

7

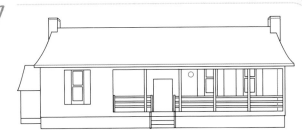

Erase the rectangular guide from step 1. Draw some of the final details on the chimney. Draw the horizontal line along the edge of the roof. Then draw the vertical line on the side of the house on the porch. Now draw the circle for the front porch light.

8

Now you are ready to shade the drawing of the house. Great job!

Meet Claudia "Lady Bird" Johnson

Claudia Alta Taylor was born on December 22, 1912, in Karnak, Texas. She was the youngest of three children born to Minnie Pattillo Taylor and Thomas Jefferson Taylor. When Claudia was a child, a nurse told her that she was as pretty as a lady bird. That is how she got the nickname "Lady Bird." From 1930 to 1934, Claudia studied

at the University of Texas at Austin. She met Johnson when he visited Austin in the fall of 1934. They married on November 17 the same year.

After Johnson became president in 1963, Lady Bird supported his programs. She headed a national campaign to make America beautiful by building parks and planting trees and flowers along highways.

Lady Bird also helped Johnson with his speeches and wrote a diary about her life in the White House. Today Lady Bird lives at the ranch in Stonewall or at her home in Austin, Texas.

1

Begin the drawing of Lady Bird Johnson with a vertical rectangle.

2

Then draw a vertical line through the middle of the rectangle. This will be your guide for drawing her body.

3

Next draw a large, tall trapezoid. This will be the lower part of Lady Bird. Then draw a smaller shape at the very top. This will be the top of her head. Then draw the oval for the face and the vertical lines for the neck.

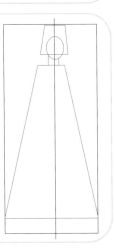

4

Begin the outline of her hair, neck, and dress collar. Draw her face, including her eyes, eyebrows, nose, and mouth.

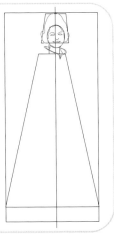

5

Now begin to draw the shoulders and arms. Draw the big fur cuffs on the sleeves of the dress. Then draw the arms and hands. Draw the line across the sleeve showing the end of the glove.

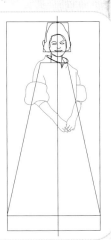

6

Next draw the bottom half of the dress and the lines running down the front of the dress.

7

Erase all the guide shapes from steps 1, 2, and 3. Begin to draw some of the final details on Lady Bird as shown.

8

Add shading and detail. Notice that her hair and the cuffs of her dress are very dark. Wonderful job!

Congressman Johnson

Lyndon Johnson was elected to the U.S. House of Representatives in 1937, a post he held until 1949. The Great Seal, which represents both Congress and the United States, is shown here. During his six terms in  Congress, Johnson made many important friends in the government. He had a friendly manner and became good at convincing others to support his projects.

When Johnson took office, the country was suffering through the Great Depression. Johnson supported President Franklin Roosevelt's New Deal programs to establish a minimum wage for workers. Johnson also helped people in rural Texas. He worked to provide electricity and running water to Texans. At that time many people in Johnson's home district did not have electricity or running water. When the United States entered World War II in 1941, Johnson briefly left Congress to serve in the U.S. Navy. He served from December 1941 to July 1942.

1 Begin the drawing of the Great Seal with a circle. Add two smaller circles inside the first circle. Draw the rectangle inside the innermost circle.

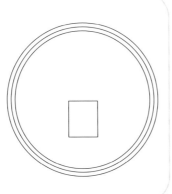

2 Draw the outline of the eagle's body as shown. Add the outline for the arrows and the olive branches the eagle holds. Add two circles above the eagle's head.

3 Draw the shield on the eagle's chest following the guide you made in step 1. In the circles above the eagle's head, draw the stars in the middle and the squiggly lines around the circles.

4 Draw the eagle's head, wings, legs, feet, and tail feathers inside the guide you made in step 2.

5 Now draw the ribbon in the mouth of the eagle. Look at the drawing to guide you. Add the olive branches and the arrows held in the eagle's feet using the guides you drew in step 2.

6 Erase extra lines. Then draw in the lines of the feathers in the wings, the neck, and the tail of the eagle. Draw the connecting lines in the middle section of the shape at the top.

7 Write the words "E PLURIBUS" on the left side of the ribbon. On the right side write "UNUM." *E Pluribus Unum* is Latin for "From many, one."

8 Shade the drawing of the Great Seal. Good work!

Johnson in World War II

The United States entered World War II on December 8, 1941, the day after Japan had attacked American ships at Pearl Harbor in Hawaii. Lyndon Johnson, who was in the Naval Reserve, reported for duty the next day.

During the next seven months, Johnson visited several islands in the South Pacific Ocean to see if the American troops stationed there had enough supplies. After he had completed this job, Johnson joined a combat mission to attack a Japanese airfield on an island in the South Pacific. On the way to the airfield, Japanese fighter planes attacked the plane in which Johnson was flying. The plane was hit, but it was able to return to its base on the island of New Guinea without any of the people aboard being hurt. For his bravery during the mission, Johnson was presented with a medal called the Silver Star, shown here. Johnson was proud of his medal and wore it often on the lapel of his jacket.

1

Start the drawing of the Silver Star medal with a vertical rectangle. This will be your guide.

2

Draw the two rectangles at the top. The smallest rectangle is the pin that LBJ wore on his lapel. Next add the shield shape and the shape below it as shown. Add the two circular shapes at the very bottom of the guide rectangle.

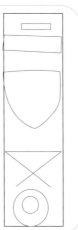

3

Draw the top of the medal using straight and curved lines. Add two curved lines to the top of the shield shape. Finish the Silver Star as shown and connect it to the shield shape using small circles and curved lines.

4

Erase extra lines in the star. Draw the lines of the smaller of the two bottom circles. Notice that it looks like a wheel. Add vertical lines in the shield-shaped ribbon above the star.

5

Add details to the lapel pin using curved and straight lines. Add straight lines to the larger rectangular part of the Silver Star medal.

6

Draw the oval-shaped wreath in the middle of the star. Then draw a smaller star in the middle of it.

7

Draw the final details inside the star using straight lines.

8

Add shading and detail to the Silver Star medal. Notice where the pin and the ribbon are striped. Great work!

Senator Johnson

In July 1942, Lyndon Johnson returned from the war to the U.S. Congress. In 1948, he campaigned for the U.S. Senate. Johnson won the election and took office in 1949.

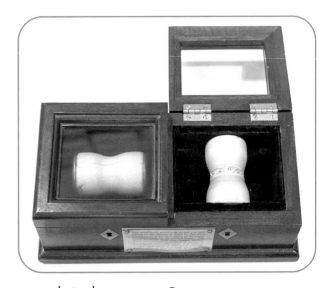

The Senate Democrats elected Johnson Senate minority leader in 1953. The minority leader is in charge of the political party that has the fewest members in the Senate. When the Democrats became the majority party in 1954, they elected Johnson the Senate majority leader. As majority leader Johnson's responsibilities included deciding when the Senate would vote on laws. Johnson controlled Senate meetings with a special gavel, shown here.

During his years in the Senate, Johnson began to work for civil rights laws that would secure equality for minority groups. Johnson was also interested in space travel. After serving in Congress for 24 years, Johnson believed that he was ready to run for president in the 1960 election.

1 Begin drawing the Senate gavel by making a rectangular guide.

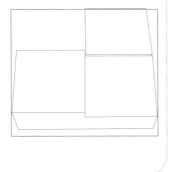

2 Now draw the three slanted square shapes. Then at the bottom draw the slanted rectangular shape connecting the two lower slanted squares.

3 Draw the inner slanted squares in all three slanted squares. This will help make the boxes the gavel rests in look deep. Then draw the shape around the bottom.

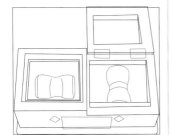

4 Draw the plaque on the gavel's box. Make sure to add the diamond shapes on either side of the plaque. Draw the gavel in the box on the left and the gavel in the box on the right. Then draw the two hinges on the box to the right between the bottom and the top rectangles.

5 Erase the rectangular guide from step 1. Erase the line through the bottom of the plaque drawn in step 4. Draw more details along the edges of the box using slanted, curved, and straight lines.

6 Add the screws to the hinges and to the front of the box. Look at the photo if you need help.

7 Add shading and detail. Notice that the lining of the box is the darkest. Wonderful job!

Becoming President

Lyndon Johnson had hoped to gain the Democratic Party's nomination for president in 1960. However, the Democrats chose John F. Kennedy as their nominee instead. Kennedy asked Johnson to be his vice president, and Johnson agreed.

After Kennedy won the presidential election, he appointed Johnson chairman of the Space Council. Johnson's most enjoyable duty as vice president was visiting other countries and meeting people from different cultures.

In November 1963, Kennedy was assassinated, and Johnson became the thirty-sixth president. He continued the programs that Kennedy had started and added some of his own. One of his programs provided health care for older people and the poor. Johnson gave funding to schools and created a program called Head Start. This program provided education for poor, preschool-age children. In 1964, Johnson ran for president and won the election.

1

Begin drawing LBJ's 1964 campaign button by making a circle.

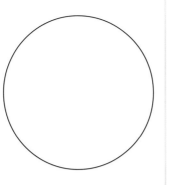

2

Draw a square inside the circle. Add a bean shape around the square. These will guide you in drawing the cowboy hat.

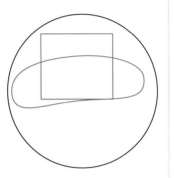

3

Draw the curves of the cowboy hat. Use the guides you drew in step 2 to help you.

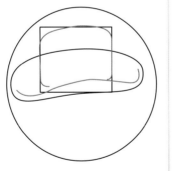

4

Erase the hat guidelines.

5

Write the letters "LBJ" in the middle of the hat.

6

Write the words "ALL THE WAY" at the bottom of the circle.

7

Draw the folds on the top of the hat.

8

Shade the campaign button. Good work!

The Civil Rights Act of 1964

Lyndon Johnson was a supporter of the civil rights movement. He believed that racial discrimination was wrong. Martin Luther King Jr., shown here, was one of the African American leaders of the civil rights movement. He supported Johnson's efforts to

pass laws that guaranteed equality for all people.

In 1964, Johnson passed the Civil Rights Act, which made segregation unlawful. Segregation is the act of keeping one group of people apart from another group. King led people in demonstrations to object to segregation.

In 1965, President Johnson passed the Voting Rights Act. This act ensured that African Americans would not be prevented from registering to vote.

Johnson's civil rights laws helped further the desegregation of schools, provide job opportunities for African Americans, and guarantee African Americans' voting rights.

1

Draw a vertical rectangle.

5

Next draw his jacket following the guides you made in step 3. Add the hand.

2

Draw the side of the stand at the bottom left corner of the box. See the drawing for details. Then draw an outline guide of the head and upper body of MLK.

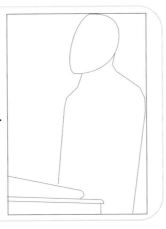

6

Erase all the guides. Draw the last details in the face. Add the button on the jacket and the last details on the stand.

3

Now draw circles for the eyes and the nose. Add a line for the mouth. Draw circles where the shoulders will be. Add oval shapes for the arm and a circle for the hand. Draw a curved line for his papers.

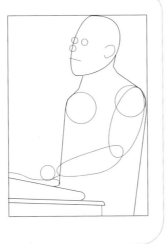

7

Draw the folds on the sleeve of his jacket using squiggly lines.

4

Begin to draw in the details for his face and head, including his hairline and ear. Draw the neck, the shirt collar, and the tie. Draw the outline of the front and back of his body.

8

You are ready to shade your drawing of Martin Luther King Jr. Great job!

The Vietnam War

The Vietnam War had begun in the early 1960s, when the North Vietnamese Vietcong soldiers attacked South Vietnam. The United States, which had promised to help the South Vietnamese, sent soldiers there in 1961. In 1964, the Vietcong attacked the USS *Maddox* in the Gulf of Tonkin near North Vietnam. The patch from the ship is shown here. After the attack Lyndon Johnson ordered the U.S. military to bomb North Vietnam. America then played an increasingly large part in the war in Vietnam.

By 1968, more than half a million American soldiers were fighting in Vietnam, and nearly 20,000 soldiers had been killed. The war was unpopular, and it affected how Americans viewed Johnson. They blamed Johnson for keeping America fighting in a costly war in which American troops were dying. The once popular Johnson was losing the support of Americans, and it led to his decision not to run for reelection in 1968.

1

You will be drawing the patch from the USS *Maddox*. Start by drawing a rectangular guide.

2

Inside the guide draw the outline of the patch as shown.

3

Next draw the inner outline of the patch. Draw the outline of the number 731 in the center of the patch.

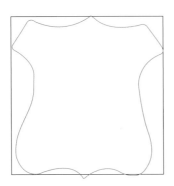

4

Begin to draw some of the shapes inside the patch. Start with the banner along the top. Add the ship in the middle as shown. Now draw the boat shape at the bottom.

5

Erase the rectangular guide you drew in step 1. Write the word "MADDOX" in the banner at the top of the patch. Draw the horizontal line just above the top ship. In the bottom half, draw the curved lines as shown.

6

Add shading and detail. Notice that the ships and the banner are the darkest. Good job!

Johnson and Space Travel

By the end of Lyndon Johnson's presidency, he wanted to boost national pride. In December 1968, the United States launched *Apollo 8*, shown here. It became the first manned spacecraft to orbit the Moon. The three astronauts onboard the spacecraft were the first people to see the dark side of the Moon. They took the first pictures of Earth from space.

Johnson supported the space program since its beginning in the 1950s. When Johnson became president, he wanted to accomplish Kennedy's goal of putting a man on the Moon by 1970. To do this he actively supported the *Apollo* program, which had begun in 1961. To honor Johnson's commitment to NASA, the U.S. space program, its headquarters for human space exploration near Houston, Texas, was renamed the Lyndon B. Johnson Space Center in 1973.

1

You will be drawing the *Apollo 8* spacecraft. Begin the drawing with a thin rectangle.

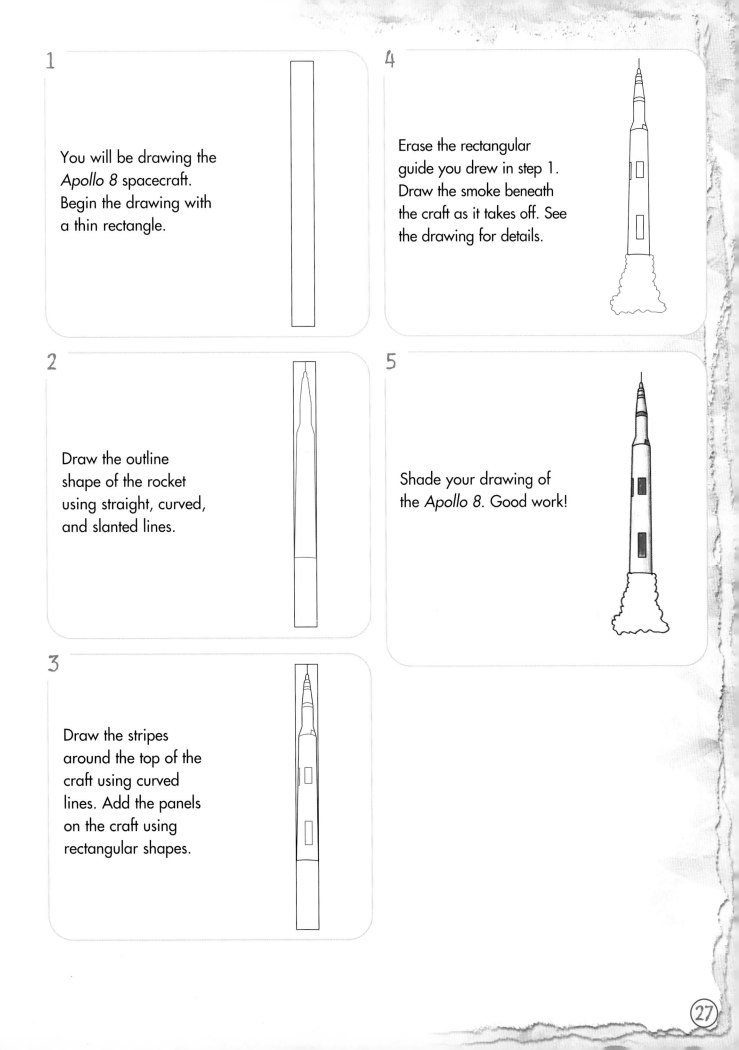

2

Draw the outline shape of the rocket using straight, curved, and slanted lines.

3

Draw the stripes around the top of the craft using curved lines. Add the panels on the craft using rectangular shapes.

4

Erase the rectangular guide you drew in step 1. Draw the smoke beneath the craft as it takes off. See the drawing for details.

5

Shade your drawing of the *Apollo 8*. Good work!

Johnson's Legacy

When Johnson left office in January 1969, he and Lady Bird retired to their Texas ranch. During the next four years, he published a book about his presidency and built his presidential library. On January 22, 1973, Johnson had a heart attack and died. He was buried on his ranch.

Johnson wanted to be remembered as a great president. Because he kept the United States in the Vietnam War, though, he went from being very popular to becoming one of the most unpopular presidents in American history. Historians are still debating Johnson's legacy, especially whether his Great Society programs were successful. The one area in which Johnson did accomplish greatness was in his fight for civil rights laws. Johnson was the first president to pass laws that guaranteed racial equality and began to bring an end to discrimination.

1

Begin the drawing of LBJ with a vertical rectangle. Then, at the bottom, draw the slanted shape as shown. These will be your guides.

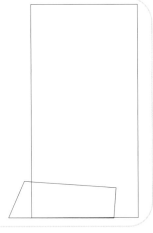

2

Draw the oval shape of the head. Draw three small circles for the eyes and the nose. Add a line for the mouth. Then draw the outline of the body and the hand.

3

Draw the outline of the head, including his hairline and ears. Add the details of his face. Next draw his neck. Add the lines of his jacket.

4

Next draw the rest of LBJ's jacket, including the lapels and the sleeves. Add the shirt collar and tie.

5

Draw the hand on the chair. Add the folds of the jacket on the right arm and on the right side of the coat.

6

Draw in the details of the chair back that LBJ is leaning against using straight and curved lines.

7

Erase the guides you drew in steps 1 and 2. Finish adding lines to LBJ's face as shown. Draw the pin on his lapel. Draw the buttons and buttonholes on his jacket.

8

Add shading and detail to your drawing of LBJ. Super job!

Timeline

1908 Lyndon Johnson is born on August 27.

1927–1930 Johnson attends Southwest Texas State Teachers College.

1931 Texas congressman Richard Kleberg appoints Johnson as his secretary.

1934 Johnson meets and marries Claudia "Lady Bird" Taylor.

1937–1949 Johnson serves in the U.S. House of Representatives.

1941–1942 Johnson serves for seven months in World War II.

1949–1961 Johnson serves in the U.S. Senate.

1953 The Democrats choose Johnson as the Senate minority leader.

1955 Johnson becomes the Senate majority leader.

1961 Johnson becomes vice president of the United States.

1963 Johnson becomes president when President Kennedy is assassinated.

1964 The Civil Rights Act is passed.
Johnson is elected president.
Johnson increases the war effort in Vietnam after the USS *Maddox* is attacked in the Gulf of Tonkin.

1965 The Voting Rights Act becomes law.

1968 *Apollo 8* orbits the Moon.
Johnson announces he will not run for reelection.

1969 Johnson retires to his ranch in Texas.

1971 The Lyndon Baines Johnson Library and Museum in Austin, Texas, opens.

1973 Johnson dies from a heart attack on January 22.

Glossary

assassinated (uh-SA-suh-nayt-ed) Killed suddenly.

civil rights (SIH-vul RYTS) The rights that citizens have.

combat (KOM-bat) Having to do with a battle or a fight.

compromise (KOM-pruh-myz) To give up something to reach an agreement.

Congress (KON-gres) The part of the U.S. government that makes laws.

cultures (KUL-churz) The beliefs, practices, art, and religion of groups of people.

declared (dih-KLAYRD) Announced officially.

demonstrations (deh-mun-STRAY-shunz) Public displays or gatherings for a person or a cause.

desegregation (dee-seh-grih-GAY-shun) The process of bringing separate groups together.

discrimination (dis-krih-muh-NAY-shun) Treating a person badly or unfairly just because he or she is different.

donated (DOH-nayt-ed) Gave something away.

Great Depression (GRAYT dih-PREH-shun) A period of American history during the late 1920s and early 1930s. Banks and businesses lost money and there were few jobs.

guaranteed (ger-un-TEED) Promised.

launched (LONCHT) Pushed out or put into the air.

legacy (LEH-guh-see) Something left behind by a person's actions.

minimum wage (MIH-nih-mum WAYJ) The lowest wage that a worker can legally be paid.

minority (my-NOR-ih-tee) The smaller part of a group or a whole.

mission (MIH-shun) A special job or task.

nomination (nah-muh-NAY-shun) The suggestion that someone or something should be given an award or a position.

poverty (PAH-vur-tee) The state of being poor.

ranch (RANCH) A large farm for raising cattle, horses, or sheep.

rural (RUR-ul) In the country or in a farming area.

Index

Web Sites

Due to the changing nature of Internet links, PowerKids Press has developed an online list of Web sites related to the subject of this book. This site is updated regularly. Please use this link to access the list:
www.powerkidslinks.com/kgdpusa/ljohnson/